NAKED STARSEED

Naked Starseed Ascension Handbook

Blood Type: Galaxy Dust

BY

Scarlet Ravin

International Best-Selling Author of "Follow the Medicine"

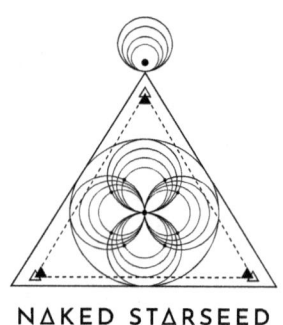

NAKED STARSEED

Ready to Ascend into Mastery?

Cover Art by Jordan Tiendas
@jordy.tiendas

Opening Prayer

The Light of Truth Shall Remind YOU

Remind you of YOUR LIGHT

Remind YOU of your Ascended Master Self

I am the container from which the Remembrance Flows through

YOU are the one Remembering

YOU are the one calling forth YOUR own LIGHT

May this book be a Star Gate for you to

REMEMBER THROUGH

Love,

Scarlet Ravin

"Extraordinary and Inspirational...I am beyond grateful for the alignment that has connected me with Scarlet. She is a lovely soul who radiates so much pure love, light and wisdom to us. Through her kindness and generosity, Naked Starseed Mystery School provides for me, a soul soothing cocoon for expression of my inner truth. Allows me to feel and be exactly who I am. Nurturing the soul and allowing me to step into my multidimensional self and BE who I truly am. Starseed on a mission...Galactic DNA activated."

-*Peggy Evans*, Naked Starseed Mystery School Student

"Scarlet's channeling of the Star Gates is opening me to the New World. When she reads the tablets, I feel the cells of my body filling with light and my consciousness being elevated. I have a long beautiful journey ahead in the Naked Starseed Mystery School and Scarlet and these words from another dimension are guiding my journey."

 -*Jill Helene*, Naked Starseed Mystery School Student

"I believe LOVE is the core. You radiate that and more into the world. Your medicine, your guidance & your healing ways are a gift for all of us."

-*Jennifer "Angel" Scott*, Naked Starseed Mystery School student

"In this transformative book, Scarlet reminds us of the power that lies within ourselves and lovingly guides us in easily accessing our own unique strength to heal and experience a joyful life. Through this book you will learn how to effectively transmute anger to love, worry to peace and helplessness to power. Scarlet is a true visionary and this book will guide you into easily stepping from the dark into the light and into peace."

-*Leah D'Ambrosio*, Naked Starseed Mystery School student

Naked Starseed Ascension Handbook; Blood type, Galaxy Dust by Scarlet Ravin

Published by Scarlet Ravin

40 Bantala Place
Castle Rock, CO 80108

www.nakedstarseed.com

Copyright © 2021 Scarlet Ravin

All rights reserved. No portion of this book may be reproduced in any form without permission from the publisher, except as permitted by U.S. copyright law. For permissions contact: scarlet@whitefoxmedicinals.com

Cover by Jordan Tiendas

Star Gate Medicine Enhanced by White Fox Medicinals, LLC
www.whitefoxnectars.com

ISBN: 9780578943862 - EBOOK
ISBN: 9780578929224 - PRINT BOOK

NAKED STARSEED

STAR GATES

The Old Earth Soul School which was covered by a dark matrix of deception has fallen. Dust it is now. Gone it is now.

What is left is a Beautiful Blank Canvas, one that is here for you to Shape the Light you wish to Shape into the Life you wish to LIVE now. Basically, it's all on you.

If you feel lower energetic emotions, it's because in your mind there is remnants of the Old Earth.

This Naked Starseed Sacred Container will be an Energetic Light Transmutation where you get to allow the denser lower vibrating frequencies come back to the light.

See this book as a Star Gate with many layers. As you turn each page you walk through another layer, this will burn away the denser energies and reveal more light of Power ready to shine from you.

Each Star Gate Is Divinely Channeled. This means that it's an embedded LIGHT CODE behind each word that resonates with your Cells and invites more light inside of YOU.

You will Awaken more and more light from each Star Gate and by the end once fully Integrated, you will Begin in the New Earth Light World of JOY, LOVE, CREATION and PLAY.

YOU are the channel where the light enters in, YOU are the Magnet of Creation Embodying your Highest Ascended master Self.

It's here.

This is a living Transmission; this book is alive. It has a Heart Beat that resonates with the Heart Beat of Source, the All-Knowing Light Shaper that we Remind ourselves we ARE now.

We are Spiraling back into the Center of our own Being, and this book is here to Hold you Dearly while you do.

HOW TO USE THIS BOOK

What you hold in your hands is a Living Ring of light manifested into book form. This book has a heartbeat, a connection to the collective and the ability to infuse you with a deeper connection to yourself and your own inner magic. Humanity is waking up, and as we awaken on a collective level many gifts are beginning to come forth from humanity.

This book is food for those gifts to grow.

There are 11 Star Gates in this book. A Star Gate is a channeled ring of light that as you read about it, the light from the words will soak into your awareness and infuse you with more light, deeper understanding and growth of your own individual empowerment.

This book is very powerful and very activating. It may be that you read one Star Gate a week and allow the light to fully integrate before you move onto the next Star Gate. It is also OK if you do not comprehend everything in this book, your soul will and your soul will enjoy the light bath.

If you feel called to move through more Star Gates then do that, always follow your own inner guidance over anything external.

No one in this world can heal anything for you, teach you anything or guide you anywhere. It's you who chooses to learn and grow yourself, it's you who heals yourself and it's you who Awakens yourself.

This book is a platform for you to do just that through this Star Gate process. This book creates a safe container for you to explore the light within on a deeper more cosmic level.

I speak to the Stars, they guide me into Ancient technologies that infuse my being with light, joy and bliss. Through this relationship the Stars taught me how to channel encoded Star Gates that I could walk through to upgrade my physical, mental and emotional bodies while charging my light body. I began to channel these Star Gates for myself and I could feel the Light in my DNA Illuminate as I did.

I began to notice my dense more challenging aspects of my life began to melt away and Joy and Bliss that I felt began to expand. I began to feel a power moving through me unlike any other that I had ever felt and once I realized that this was a Portal for not just me, but for everyone I began to share the Star Gates in my Naked Starseed Mystery School. This Ascension container receives a new video recorded Star gate each week and the students get to walk through them with me as I channel them.

The students began to feel the light cover them and enhance their lives as well which led me to writing this book to share more Star Gates with more beings who are ready to stand in their Empowerment of Light and feel the Creator being come forth and shape the New Earth.

Some Star Gates may make you tired, requesting that you sleep deeply for integration. Some Star Gates may give you bountiful energy! Some may trigger you as you bring dense energy to the surface for transmutation and some may feel like nothing.

All experiences with the Star Gates are perfect for you just as you feel them. There is no duality of right or wrong in this Ascension process there is only the opportunity for you to experience deeper aspects of yourself. Discover deeper gifts hidden within you and enlighten aspects of your beings so that you may excel through your Ascension process.

My Soul Gift is to offer these Star Gates to the Collective and with a deep bow of gratitude I offer these channelings to you from the depth of my heart. I am devoting myself to you as I know, we are actually one. We are not separate. The more light I share with the collective the more light I share with myself. We are all woven into one blanket of conscious energy!

Enjoy these bountiful rings of light here to awaken your gifts and inner glow, I love you!

Star Gates

Star Gate 1- Witness through Source Eyes
Star Gate 2- Anchor to the Body – Grounded Embodiment
Star Gate 3- Elemental Fae Realm Star Gate
Star Gate 4- Abundance Magnetism – Moon Gifts Implant
Star Gate 5- Sexual Blooming - Earth and Star Channels
Star Gate 6- Link to the Unseen
Star Gate 7- Innocence Embodiment – Free of Fear
Star Gate 8- Story time Star Gate – Connection to Source
Star Gate 9- Innovation – Trust of Self
Star Gate 10- LOVE
Star Gate 11- Mastery- Create your own Star Gates

NAKED STARSEED

<u>Star Gate 1</u>
Witness through Source Eyes

Remember when your consciousness was fully meshed with the consciousness of source while you were in the womb before birth? You were the great experience of vibrations, the great witness to the unfolding of Evolution.

This being in the womb knows this: There is nothing wrong with you, there is nothing that needs to be fixed. You are not broken and you do not need to change anything about yourself. You are created in the likeness of Source, this can never be separated.

Once you came into this world you were surrounded by beings who had forgotten this and began boxing different experiences into two boxes, good boxes and bad boxes. This gave birth to duality in your mind and this duality allowed you to dive deeper and deeper into who you are from the inside out. You are able to play in the realm of duality to give you deeper fuel into creating the reality you desire. Duality is the foundation for you discovering your desires, your desires is what creates worlds.

This is a beautiful thing. This Star Gate you are about to walk into is going to deepen the understanding of Source Eyes, so you may upgrade how you move into your desires. You need no longer move into your desires via duality, you can move into them via Witnessing.

The witness see's what is happening all around them and inside of them and see's all of this activity as Divinity. There is no good or bad experience, only opportunities to sink deeper into what one is experiencing and it is through this deepening that you will discover the Beauty and Life in any experience. Source is always present in all things in all ways, when you walk through this Star Gate on the other side you will integrate Source Eyes into your daily Experiencing.

These Source Eyes give you the opportunity to enter into a resistance free state no matter what is happening, the object of this view point is it feeds you life force. It dissolves all layers of armory around the soul and creates a pathway back to your ability to observe and experience just as you did in the womb state with the added bonus of having walked through duality as well. You get both!

Once you Embody Source Eyes of Witnessing, you are able to claim all of your power in any experience. You are able to shape light into what you want automatically as you walk through this world without any resistance to any experience.

It is from this vibrational resonance that you are living a multidimensional reality in your ascended form. This perspective gives you all your soul is seeking, gives you access to the depth of every living moment in its entirety. Ready?

"I seek Abundance, Clarity and Miracles as everyday moments. I seek the pulsating endless connection to Source and all the Wisdom of the universe to be offered to me in each moment. I seek connecting to the unseen realms in all moments so I may always walk through this world through the eyes of source.

I walk through this ring of light, I walk through this pulsating Activation to awaken the parts of myself that have fallen asleep since I was born. I invite this seed of Awakening back into my conscious awareness now. I allow the Eyes of Source to Integrate into physical form now so I may have access to this high view of sight.

I witness my DNA illuminating deeper in this conscious upgrade I am creating for myself. I see myself witnessing moments in time with no judgment, no emotional charge. I have mastered the art of being soft and allowing the experiences to move through me so I may feel them

at the depth of my soul. I will be moved by each miracle before me all the time.
I allow this remembrance to take root now.

The vibrational resonance of judgement, bad, good and having to understand the root of things is dissolving in my being. They are of low vibrational frequencies and I make a conscious choice to no longer carry them with me in my being or in my fields around me. I release them fully to the wind now and I allow the upgrade to fully integrate, now that I have said goodbye to my density.

I am grateful for the lessons taught by this duality, and I see now how evolving past this is obtaining higher viewpoints, viewpoints as Source would see it.

This allows me to feel all moments in time and KNOW the beauty in the seed of each moment. This allows me to revel in the bliss of each tiny happening and tie these miracles into a web of experiences for me on this earth and beyond.

I am fully aware that as I upgrade my vibrational resonance to this knowing I am adding a significant amount of light and evolution to the collective net of consciousness therefor picking up my brothers and sisters into a higher realm of understanding also. I see that knowing this in each moment is a part of having Source Eyes now.

Thank you for my new lens from the vibrational resonance of source. I look forward to testing out this new higher vibrational outlook on my life experience. I am excited to Embody this new sight by practicing it every day in my own being so that I anchor it into form with my free will.

I vow to practice this in each moment, to shape my mind to see only in this way and to do so with a passion for Ascended Mastery unlike this world has yet to see! I am the light I seek and I am grateful for a deeper merger into this Knowing now!"

This Star Gate came through as a reflective mirror of the Source inside of you. This is why it is spoken as if you are speaking this. Read this one more time with this knowing in your mind, you are the one speaking this upgrade to yourself. You are the one awakening cells filled with light in this time by being Aware that you can. Practice this, reread this and know that anything you wish to evolve into is at your command, just as you experienced this Star Gate.

I love you.

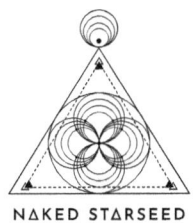

Star Gate 1 Anchor into the Physical

Allow what you experienced to pour onto these pages. As you shape this light into form by writing it on these pages you begin to Embody this Wisdom in your own Temple. Once you reach Embodiment this Wisdom is Awakened inside of you. Writing is your first step into Embodiment.

NAKED STARSEED

Star Gate 2
Anchor to the Body – Grounded Embodiment

When this world speaks of Temples, the story feels Sacred. These Sacred sites were anchored into the Earth and given prayers, devotional architecture, embedded codes for higher powers and more. They are beautiful, glorious and Inspire us to be more devoted to our own God Like Essence. Each culture has a different version of this sacred temple, and each vibe is just as stunning.

Did you know you have your own Sacred Temple gifted to you during Incarnation? Did you know this Sacred Site is the Seat of your very own Soul? Your Body. Your Sacred Temple site is Your Body, your Physical incarnation here anchored to the Heart Beat of Mother Gaia and open to the Guidance from Father Sun. Your Sacred Temple is a conduit where the stars get to kiss the Earth through your feet, where the Sun gets to guide his children into ever growing higher states of light embodiment, as he is the King of Light Embodiment is he not?

Your Sacred Temple, once recognized as such becomes an Anchor where you can store all of your Source given powers ready to wield as you chose! Inside your sacred Temple is rings of many light codes that are ready to share infinite wisdom, guidance and healing with you now.

In every cell of your Temple is the knowledge, magic and life of all that is and all that has ever been. Inside your temple is the pathway to every enlightened state you seek to embody and every pathway to the Desire filled life you wish to create.   Your Temple is the Main Star Gate for you in this world, in this lifetime. Once connected to the depth of this knowing you'll have access to unimpeded power that you can will into anything you wish for the greater good for all.

Our brother Jesus knew this, our brother Buddha knew this, as well as our Mother Mary and her beloved Mary Magdalene. They all knew the physical body was the Anchor for all power to manifest through. It's through this intimate connection to self every other power you have gets harnessed and amplified to serve you and the rest of the planet and galaxies.

Ready to walk through this Star Gate? Where this light code of prayers will awaken you to this remembrance?

Ok Ascended Master, let's go!

"Allow me to tickle your physical sense with this light encoded transmission, step into my ring of light dear one's and I shall begin to kiss your skin with my loving light. I am here to burn away all dense energies off of your Temple that resemble disconnection from your Physical Temple.

I am here to remind you of the Sacredness of your body and how this is the foundation for you to Embody your Ascended Mastery here in this Life Time Now. Your skin dances with this reality around you and feeds you sensations. It's the vibrations of these senses that remind you, YOU ARE ALIVE! This is a fact that is beyond any magic we could share. You are in a body, on the planet and you are alive! This transmission may be the most important moment to Remember. It takes a BRAVE Soul to come to Earth School, to Evolve itself and Share ore light, and you chose this path. You chose to incarnate into a Physical Body that would guide you back to Ascended Mastery in order to expand consciousness again, and again and again.

Your Divine Soul chose this pathway, and this is a Miracle here to be honored for what it is. If you have a body and your alive inside of it, you're Brave, you're Devoted to Higher Light and you are a Leader in Expansion of Consciousness. You chose this physical body as the perfect Ascension Vehicle for you to come back into your Mastery.

You designed every aspect of your Temple because you knew this would be a grounded catalyst that would give you every opportunity to accomplish your Soul's Mission in this lifetime.

Therefor, your Temple is perfection from Source here to awaken your Destiny of Embodiment of Ascended Mastery. Say that three times fast!

Also, keep this affirmation close to you, repeat it often. It's a light code for oneness with the Body Temple:

My Temple is Perfection from Source here to Awaken My Destiny of Embodiment of my Ascended Mastery.

This is a huge remembrance. Sit with this before you move on deeper into this Star Gate. Pausing to fully inhale a new Transmission is walking a pathway that respects the pace of the Temple. Your Temple has a speed it wishes to go in in order to really be able to absorb fully the magic all around it. Begin to practice what pace feels best to your temple and when. Begin to strengthen that link between you and your Divine Body. You are Source Perfection so now we shall burn away the external input that swayed you to think otherwise.

Here comes the most perfect little baby, she was just born. Her smile lights up a room and her connection to her body is like swimming in sensations, it's all perfectly witnessed and felt to the depth of her soul. She knows she is perfect, she knows she is Source here to play with the expansion of light. She dances in this bliss of connection to her Temple, she listens to everything it needs and expresses that to other's as soon as she is aware of it. The sensations in her body is her guide of devotion and everything she does is completely connected to what's best for her Temple.

Around her are lower vibrating realities that say the body is not that important, and it is certainly not perfect. The body is to heavy, to thin, so weak. The body is so vulnerable and so hard to understand.

She feels these energetic impressions around her and from her perspective, it's hilarious. She KNOWS her body is perfection, there is no room for any other impression at this time for the sensations that envelope her earth experience are directly derived form this temple, there is no other way to experience this earth in this way. Her body is the Star Gate into Life itself! Without this Portal there would be no experiencing so how off kilter to judge the very portal Star Gate that ALLOWS you to experience this glory of this planet? How odd to embody a thought that would say your own personal Star Gate is less than that of the light of Source?

It's literally absurd.

The only reason those vibrational rings of disconnection are here around your initial perfection is so that you can feel the connection of your own Temple Body even deeper. So that you can not only know how Divine your body is but you can Know how it's the God of your own Ticket to being here on this planet, and it is to be honored as such.

When you begin to Remember this, and Honor your Physical body as the Star Gate to all life for you to create this Multidimensional relationship to your own body. You begin to look at your body as the impulses run through you and guide you to what to nourish it with, guide you to what it needs in terms of rest or play. You begin to look at your Body as a Temple of Divinity that is to be treated as such.

Would you go into a Sacred Temple and begin to comment on how the colors are all wrong? The size is totally off? How the landscaping around it sucks? How the height of the walls are so lacking?

No.

You'd honor the presence of the Divine you feel inside of it and allow this to be an experience for you.

Your body is that same experience for you each and every moment to where your walking through a Divine Star Gate of Sensational Experiences in each moment you have breathe inside of you and this is to be honored as the miracle it is.

You are reconnecting this remembrance for yourself right now as you expand your awareness by reading this Living Codex. Feel yourself expand into the knowing of how Sacred your body is. Feel the sensations pumping through you now that you realize how much power you really do have in your finger tips.

Feel the Strands of DNA alight inside of you while you ponder this Sacred Portal you have just walked through. Allow the depth of expansion to be embodied by feeling what the body feels, becoming one with your temple once again.

This is what you truly are. A walking Temple of Divinity in motion shaping light into new Worlds to experience more sensations of light. This is your essence and it's anchored into your Physical Body. Enjoy Beloved!"

Lay upon the Earth and ask her to massage this Ascended remembrance into the depths of your cells. Ask her grounded depth to vibrate through you so you may resonate with the vibration of mother earth and Embody this Star Gate even deeper. The Sacredness that is you is here to be Embodied, and this is what you came here to do.

I love you.

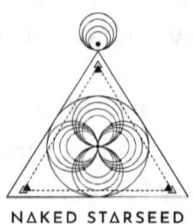

NΔKED STΔRSEED

Star Gate 2 Anchor into the Physical

Allow what you experienced to pour onto these pages. As you shape this light into form by writing it on these pages you begin to Embody this Wisdom in your own Temple. Once you reach Embodiment this Wisdom is Awakened inside of you. Writing is your first step into Embodiment.

NΔKED STΔRSEED

Star Gate 3
Elemental Fae Realm Star Gate

There is an invitation of Power resting at your heart. This Invitation intertwines all of the Elemental Powers of this Earthly Realm and it swirls this magic into Your Very Own DNA.

This Dance of Connection between the Rhythm of the Earth and us Humans is one of the most Natural Essence of All Time. Forgetting is ok, as for now it's time to Remember this Relationship.

The Elemental Kingdom carries inside of it a Connection to Earth, Air, Wind, Fire Essence and it also connects you to every Plant, Natural Essence of Medicine from the Earth as well as all Sprites, Fairies and other Elemental Beings here to Weave Earth Heart Beat into Each Breathe we Take.

As ONE we Remember this.

Why do we LOVE to surround ourselves with Himalayan Salt Lamps? They remind us of this Connection, when the air coming off of our Skin is illuminated by the Conscious Relationship of EVERYTHING.

Elemental Fae Realm Star Gate:

"I Sing to you softly with my voice all aglow, I whisper sweet everything's deep in your ear. Your Heart Is My Heart and my Gifts are you, I am the Mystical Friend sticking to you like Glue.

I am ready to deepen this Connection between us, so it is time you matched me in this Passion. My Gifts are YOUR Gifts, if you wish them to be. Everything I can do is for you to harness. Do you wish to be the Wind my love? Imprint my gifts onto you. Do you Wish to be the Water knowing ALL impressions of ALL time? Speak to me from the Heart my LOVE and all of me is yours.

I can Burn away the Dense Realms from past times, I can Breathe Fresh Air up and down your Spine. Together we can increase the growth in the plants, while weaving back each and every animal Chant. This Rhythm is in the depth of your Heart, as you step through this Star Gate you Align with ALL PARTS.

You are illuminated from within the core of your being, you are washing yourself with the Golden Rainbow Light Body of Mastery. Every Element ALL around you, is filled with Enchanted Gifts. Now you know, if you wish to increase your POWERS and Harness this Wisdom, you are now open, Aligned and Activated to Do so.

As you complete the last few steps of this Elemental Star Gate, your Essence sinks into a state of Deep Relaxation, Rhythmic Holding by Mother Earth and a Nation of Stars coming through your Crown.

You have chosen to Initiate Yourself back into Harmony with this Elemental Kingdom, therefor Harvesting a Deeper Glow of the Truth of YOU.

Finish this Integration by Playing with and Speaking Directly to the Elements. Play with them, Dance with them and Remember to Imprint their Gifts upon YOU."

This abundantly filled Star Gate is here for YOU Always, in All ways. It's time to step into nature and feel the Tree's Wisdom enter into the Depths of Your Heart. It is time for you to now go forth and live by your words of Devotion to the Elements that shower you with Gifts. Walk in this Prayer of Thanks and Watch the World Inside Fire A Glow.

I love you

Star Gate 3 Anchor into the Physical

Allow what you experienced to pour onto these pages. As you shape this light into form by writing it on these pages you begin to Embody this Wisdom in your own Temple. Once you reach Embodiment this Wisdom is Awakened inside of you. Writing is your first step into Embodiment.

Star Gate 4
Abundance Magnetism, Moon Gift Implant

You LOVE this light of silky glowing lavender, I know you do. It soothes your body, mind and soul. This Lavender is what you may see right now as you walk up to me however soon I will show you the origins of this glow. Come closer to me until you can feel the heat of my light dance upon your skin. Now invite my Glow into you…Softly…Sweetly…With an Open Heart. As if you were inviting a Lover into Your Bedroom.

Breathe me in. Drink me in. From each cell of your body draw me inside of you, allow this breathing in of my Lavender Glow to magnetize you towards me so you effortlessly float into my Star Gate.

You are drawing me in, as the Moon draws the tide with her Magnet. You are Drinking me in as the moon drinks in the emotions she stirs up. You are opening every part of your body to me as if we have been by one another's side since the beginning of all Creation.

Now can you see me? Glowing in front of you? I am the moon. I am the greatest Magnet known to all the Galaxies. Magnetism was invented by witnessing my Powers upon the Earth. Whatever I want I draw to me with an open-hearted loving reunion of all that is.

Would you like my Gifts? Would you like to have my Powers so you may will your Magnetism upon this life? Ask and they are yours.

Ask now and I will imprint my gifts into your DNA and you will awaken to this magnetism that rests in the Center of your Stomach. Your Power Center. Shall we turn on this Magnet inside of your stomach?

The process has begun now that you have affirmed YES. You are drawing me in deeper allowing me to enter into the depths of YOU. I am you and you are me, my gifts are now your gifts.

Breathe into the depths of your Stomach and feel the Lavender Glow emanate from the center of your Stomach. Allow the open portals in your hands to absorb this Lavender Glow into them and activate additional power centers in the Palms of your Hands.

Now move your hands to your heart, allow this Lavender Glow to enter into the core of your heart and upgrade all internal powers now. Breathe this in deeply.

Gently slide your hands up to your throat center, open the heart of your throat and allow this lavender Light to dance into your Speech, magnetizing your Light Language and Giving you the ability to attract in with your words, now. Breathe this in Deeply.

Move your palms up to your Third Eye center and allow the Lavender light flowing from your palms to swirl into your Third Eye now. Breathe this Lavender Light in and see your Powers of Bringing in all the Visions called forth awaken. See this powerful inner tool glow with Ascended Mastery in the World of Visions now. Breathe this in deeply.

Breathe in as you move your hands up to the crown of your head. Allow the Lavender Liquid to flow into your crown and overflow spilling down your face and back of your neck. See this light beginning to travel all over the surface of your body as you move your hands down to your Sexual Portal right below your belly button.

Breathe in this Liquid Lavender light as it flows over your skin, into your crown and now enters into your sexual power center filling your sacred pleasures with a fulfilling magnetism that nourishes the soul, body and mind. Breathe this in deeply.

With a closing prayer bring your hands to your root center, where the grounding cord of your being comes out of your body to head down to the center of Mother Earth. See the Lavender light flowing into your grounding cord and travel up your spine meeting the light coming down your crown. You are filled with a liquid Lavender light of magnetism in an endless glow of Power.

As I leave you, I leave a part of my Blue Print in the Center of your Stomach to always keep you connected to the original source of your magnetism. We shall pulse as one now, mother and child here to amplify and support one another into stepping into our greatest potential.

Together we Ascend.

I love you.

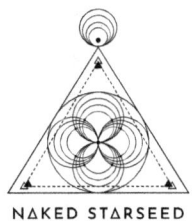

Star Gate 4- Anchor into the Physical

Allow what you experienced to pour onto these pages. As you shape this light into form by writing it on these pages you begin to Embody this Wisdom in your own Temple. Once you reach Embodiment this Wisdom is Awakened inside of you. Writing is your first step into Embodiment.

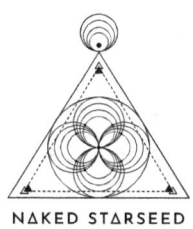

Star Gate 5
Sexual Blooming – Earth and Star Channels

Sex. All beings have a natural draw to the Sexual Energies of their system as the Soul knows this is the Power Center of Creation when it is aligned with certain other aspects of self. This Star Gate is an alignment back to this Powerful Current waiting to be unleashed to you so you may amplify your powers of Creation.

Sexual energy begins in the sexual centers, there are channels running up and down the spine that swirl up to the base of the skull, then drip their powers into further illuminating a person's magnetic field when the foundation for this to occur is aligned.

The first component that is to be seen is safety in the heart. Trust in the Heart and Safety In the heart. It's is from this Vibrational Resonance one can awaken the depth of their Sexual Power and channel this into their Life for Creating, Healing and Amplifying Bliss, which is your birthright.

Safety is the warm pink glowing cocoon that is directly connected to the sexual power center and the depth of the heart center. When this cocoon of light is fully intact, meaning the being feels safe, and can trust then this glow brightens. From this channel the heart is invited to open to the depths of magic hidden inside the seed of Source itself. The heart must feel Safe to fully open, and the heart must be fully open to open the channel for the sexual energy to reach the top of the crown then spill over in a bath of powerful healing light.

This Powerful healing Sexual light has the ability to heal all disease, awaken Awareness, Attract in any Manifestation as well as boost you into your full Ascended Master Self. This practice can evolve into a practice of Ascension, where you ritually create this powerful flow of energy and you channel it through your own systems in order to burn away all dense energies and lift you into an Enlightened State.

Many beings before us used this, Jesus and Mary used this practice to obtain Enlightenment. Mary's Magnetic womb was the light source that charged Jesus light body so he may awaken as an Ascended Master and live forever in this state.

We can practice this alignment alone first and this is very encouraged as it helps you embody this practice before you add another humans energy to the experience.

This Star Gate is an Activation into this State of Knowing about your sexual power and the opportunity before you to practice this channeling. You must flex this muscle and practice in order for this Powerful Energy to be a part of your embodiment. It is through the practice you anchor this into the cells of your being and over time you emanate this exotic light field that is able to awaken anyone around you. Heal anyone around you and also guide you into each creation you desire fully held in abundance.

Breathe this in deeply and prepare for this Sexual Star Gate which will align you with trust, safety, and unconditional love so you may explore this opportunity more deeply from a place of awakening.

"I am a bright light Star Gate, this I know. I am also a very soothing Star Gate which is what surprises most beings as they associate sex with red and fire. The red and fire is within me as well, however it is only balanced with Safety and Trust. It is balanced with an open heart and unconditional love pouring forth.

When you can mix this powerful sexual energy with these other vibrational aspects you receive floods of energy up your spine, into your crown that spills over in a Rainbow Light body Blessings bringing you closer and closer to your Ascended Mastery.

Here is your Key to Embodiment: Softness.

Breathe. Become Softness. Become the nurturing love from Mother Mary, become the relaxed gaze of a sleeping cat. Become the softness of the clouds above. From this place you can feel the parts of your system that may not feel safe. Speak to them, acknowledge them with Love pouring from your heart. Do this until you feel all that is aching to be seen has been seen in this moment.

Now you have invited all of you into this moment which allows you to become even softer. Your Heart asks if you could please place your hand upon it. Feel her beat into your hand, feel her pulse her love into your hand and feel this pulse spread love throughout your whole body. Continue this practice daily relinking yourself to your own source of unconditional love.

Once you have done this over the course of several days this will awaken and feed the trust of self you have inside. This trust of self will vibrate out and attract in beings that will be trust worthy of your open heart. This will feed into you having experiences from an open heart, with a safe container where you can then open up to sexual energy. From this container anything is possible.

Anyone can rub their sexual parts into another person and feel pleasure. This is about upgrading that Pleasure into a pathway into the center of your soul, and to have this upgrade occur your heart must approve. This happens over time. Your heart has its own pathway to wholeness and your softness and presence with love will bring you back into 100% alignment so you may become enlightened through this practice.

This Star Gate you have just walked through with your awareness has planted seeds that this alignment has already occurred into every cell of your body. You have all that you need to embody this knowing now. Practice and it will come into your life sooner then you expect."

This is a Powerful Star Gate, it has opened you up to a road that will take you to fully illuminating your Light body or Ka body. It is from this place we no longer experience life and death cycles, but we live from our light body into the rest of our existence. The sun also charges your light body, doing this practice in the Sun will help you amplify this embodiment.

I love you.

NΔKED STΔRSEED

Star Gate 5- Anchor into the Physical

Allow what you experienced to pour onto these pages. As you shape this light into form by writing it on these pages you begin to Embody this Wisdom in your own Temple. Once you reach Embodiment this Wisdom is Awakened inside of you. Writing is your first step into Embodiment.

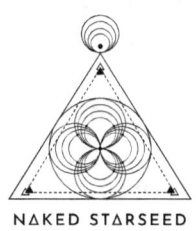

NAKED STARSEED

Star Gate 6
Link to the Unseen

There is a tiny moment in time before everything comes into form. A moment where a seed begins to take root in the unseen worlds and dances before you like an option of desire. YOU are the one that shapes the roots of this manifestation.

YOU are the one that once you remember how to see this moment in time, before things become into form how to interact with this light and shape it into what you DESIRE in that MOMENT.

This Star Gate reminds you of how to flex that creator muscle, not through the force of the Physical but by the attunement to the non-physical from which all springs forth.

The Star Gate is before you is illuminated. You can see light dancing forth from the ring it creates, giving you a warmth upon your skin. As you walk up to Star Gate 1 your body feels tingles of Remembrance, Excitement and Desire to know your Own Light more.

You allow this Desire to know your own light grow inside of you. You allow it to start to flood the cells of your body, you begin to breathe it deeply in, you expand it consciously inside of you.

Now that you have expanded it, you begin to feel a close resonance with the Physical Star Gate in front of you and you begin to feel a magnetic pull towards it, as if you were about to become one with it.

The layers of light begin to engulf you, begin to surround you until all you feel, hear and see is light. Your physical body begins to feel as if it is floating, yet fully tethered to the core of Mother Earth. The wisdom from the Stars begins to pour into you now and you hear this:

"I am you and you are me. There is no space between us. We dance as one light form or another always changing, as we are dynamic. We play in the realm of Source, Zero Point Field Energy. We dance into each one of your Cells as I am you, and you are ME. There is no separation you see.

You can feel me touch your skin, you can also feel me glow from within. You can feel me stroke your head, and you can feel me carry you to bed. I am you and you are me, there is no separation you see."

Allow this light language to seep deeply into you, allow the light inside. Allow it to engulf you and encourage the magnetism of more light to you now.

From this place, you can now see what I speak of, this place of unseen creation before something comes into form. This feeling you feel engulfed by the light is the Resonance connection to that space in time where you can shape the light in front of you into any experience you wish to create.

This feeling, this light bath of love is what you rest in now to fully remember your connection to this Ability, of Receptivity.

The Realm of Creation Springs Forth from the Realm of Light Receptivity. Breathe this in.

You have now walked through Star Gate 1. Take time to integrate this Remembrance, allow a long salt bath to relax the systems, and have a long nice sleep. Drink plenty of water, stay away from Electronics and allow the Earth to hold you. If your Naked that's even better. There is Power in Being Naked on the Earth, and this Power Shall help you Integrate All.

I love you.

Star Gate 6- Anchor into the Physical

Allow what you experienced to pour onto these pages. As you shape this light into form by writing it on these pages you begin to Embody this Wisdom in your own Temple. Once you reach Embodiment this Wisdom is Awakened inside of you. Writing is your first step into Embodiment.

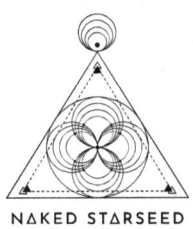

NAKED STARSEED

Star Gate 7
Innocence – Free of Fear

Welcome to the Star Gate of Remembered Innocence, an Illumination that basks in the Light of your Divine Beginning. When you came into this world as Pure Source form you easily recalled and moved from a place of Innocence. Wide open eyes, here to discover with an innate sense of curiosity what it's like to interact with a world such as Earth. Your cells pulsed with the rhythm of Gaia, your crown resonated with the rhythm of Star Light and your heart was wide open, reaching for more and more love to share with every breathe.

This is YOU. This vibrational element of Innocence is what you are at your root. This Innocence resonates with a white lily gently blowing in the wind, or a baby horse running through the field towards her mother. A divine picture of all that is bliss, presence and love in this world.

This Star Gate that you will walk through will Transmute back to the light any and all rings of Fear resonance that distract you from this natural state of being. YOU are not what you have been through, you are not a being who resonant with fear naturally and you are not in need of protection.

Breathe deeply into the core of your being and fully arrive in the Divine Presence of your body. It is from this place you can request that you naturally sink back into your foundational alignment of innocence and allow this Star Gate to burn off into the light all resonance with fear. Breathe deeply, allow your belly to fill. These breathes you take are light baths for your cells, breathe is pure source energy. Breathe.

Your Awareness now remembers about your natural state of existence, Innocence. You are embodying that Ascended knowing now. Come with me now and we shall transmute any lingering fear paradigms that have long since lost their use in this New Earth.

"Innocence ring of light I am. I am embedded with Unconditional love. My very heated presence casts a warm glow of held love into your experience now. Like you are being wrapped in a warm blanket of light, held by Mother Mary. Feel the warm slowly steep into each of your cells and wash through them with a warm yellow hue glow. Feel the relaxation this initiates into your experience, and how this naturally opens the Heart.

There is a softness to your state of mind, which allows a fluid river of creative wonder to come alive from the center of your heart. You feel your light expand with a pulse wave from each heart beat. You allow this creative wonder to envelop you and begin to guide you. Each spark of curiosity is innately linked to your heart field and magnetically draws you into experiences of Trust, Exploration and Creation into this world.

You create new entire multiverses in your minds eye, you can feel the different climates these new planets have and you can feel the strength and bravery rushing through your veins as you create entirely new worlds. These new worlds are your playgrounds, you have entered into your creator state while being held in a river of fluidity from Source. Your only job is to explore, create and feel what this experience is lie for you.

Your presence is deeply connected to each moment as you go deeper and deeper in to the creating. Your cells are now aligned with the Fire of Innocence. You are standing in the full embodiment of Eyes of a Child. You are fresh, Powerful, Brave and Playful.

From this vibrational Stance, turn and look at the parts of your being that used to hold the resonance of fear, limiting beliefs and external input of misunderstanding. Invite them all to look you in your eyes, gaze at them all with unconditional love, as from this perspective, the Eyes of a Child Innocence Perspective You Transmute these old energetic paradigms into light, burning them out of your experience and allowing the lessons they gave you to be fully integrated now.

There is no need for fear or protection in this New Earth you are here to create. There is no room for past hurts to be continually carried into the future in this New Earth now. The New Earth is your playground of Creation. It is the place where you embody your innocence having made a full circle in the journey of your lifetime now.

You Journeyed through the density, the fear. You experienced that. Now it's time to move on, to leave what you know behind and begin to be open to what you can create for yourself now.

This Innocence is you, there is zero separation between you and this abundant Mother Mary Unconditionally Loving light."

The strength of you has stepped out of what was and remembered your birth right. Innocence. You have created an opportunity to experience this purity once again, now with the awakening of many lessons and gifts at your fingertips as well. You have the power of Source beyond when you stand In the power of Innocence. You are held, amplified and loved deeply, always.

It is you who has called in this upgrade, a return to Innocence.

I love you.

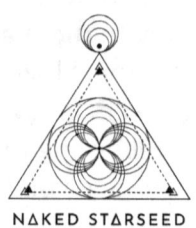

NAKED STARSEED

Star Gate 7- Anchor into the Physical

Allow what you experienced to pour onto these pages. As you shape this light into form by writing it on these pages you begin to Embody this Wisdom in your own Temple. Once you reach Embodiment this Wisdom is Awakened inside of you. Writing is your first step into Embodiment.

Star Gate 8
Story Time Star Gate – Connection to Source

Your worth is that of Source, you are Made in the Likeness of the Grand Creator of All things. Feelings of unworthiness, or lack stem from a dense energy that is now dead. It's up to us to lay this energy down for transmutation back to the light. It is up to us if we wish to feed this old energy in the thoughts inside of our mind. Externally, on this New Earth platform there is no such thing as self-worth.

All that is left is the Remembrance of Connection to Source, inside of this Remembrance is the Knowing you are Source.

Story Time Star Gate #2.

There is a Glowing Star Gate of Remembrance before you, this Star Gate contains Codes of Awakening for your DNA, very soon you shall come back into contact with the Resonance of Source. Inside of this Resonance the word Worthy cannot exist, for we are stepping into the New Earth where everything emanates Source and warms one's Heart. No Division, Means No Worth to have an UnWorthy counterpart.

Star Gate #2 is a Story Time Star Gate. She Glows with a bright white light which blinds your eyes so you must look inside. You begin to breathe her light in more deeply as you feel an integration occur with the amplification offered. From this sustained illuminated state, you listen to this Star Gate's Story:

"My words are prayers upon your heart. You know me, Your Cells Know me, your DNA Remembers me. I am the light from which all came from and when I made you, I took a Particle of Light from me, and I expanded it. The very beginning of you came from the Heart of me, therefore Starseed, You are ME.

You are not just the likeness of me, YOU are ME.

When you say, I AM, you are Resonating with the Mastery Resonance of this Star Gate.

You have taken this seed of Light I created you from and you have nurtured it and held it in LOVE. This has given that light a new Shape, the Shape YOU chose it to become. This play ground for you here on EARTH is a platform to shape the light you were made from. To take what I did to create you and for you to create from that place.

See? See how you are me? See how you're doing what I did to create you? See how the circle of knowing deeply oneself is you coming home to me? The Source of All Creation and All that is? See?

I know you See, I can feel you Knowing what I share. I can feel you absorbing my light beyond the words of this page and I can see how you see this book as a glowing ring of light that is bouncing around your heart in a cosmic awakening. I can see all of this inside of you.

Rest. Rest in this Knowing, PLAY. Play will bring you home to me, for all I do is PLAY, Create and LOVE you.

Remember, YOU are ME and I YOU."

From this Resonance we rest, we rest and we expand.

Now YOU Integrate. Rest. Relax. Be...

If you Forget come back home, however you will never forget again, as this is the New Earth all that is here is all that Never Was Before.

I love you.

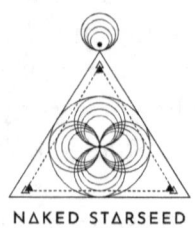

Star Gate 8- Anchor into the Physical

Allow what you experienced to pour onto these pages. As you shape this light into form by writing it on these pages you begin to Embody this Wisdom in your own Temple. Once you reach Embodiment this Wisdom is Awakened inside of you. Writing is your first step into Embodiment.

NAKED STARSEED

Star Gate 9
Innovation – Trust of Self

How does one connect with the Rings of light around them holding new inventions for this planet to bring forth?

Ask yourself this question now.

Answer?

By asking the question. Do you feel yourself embedded with light? Do you feel how asking this question gave rise to your resonance? YOU are the Creator of this felt experience you feel, and by asking questions of Innovation you are saying to Source, "I Desire to Enlighten myself and the Planet even Further."

Every Desire you carry in your heart is a connection to something greater. Something beyond what has ever been and your true soul seeds that rest inside of your being are here to grow new worlds of light. New ways of being. New ways of thinking and obtaining light. New mechanisms for expansion.

These codes of Invention are not only inside of every cell of your being, they are also vibrating in rings around you ready to be accessed at any time. You can call them in and your inner cellular vibration will awaken and share with you new insights, innovations to change the world and feelings you will be able to embody to create this new world of Light.

Star Gate to Innovation? Ready...

"What a Glow you already are! Filled with divinity, the codes in this Star Gate will awaken your Ascended mastery to the level of Authenticity it requires for true alignment with Body, Mind and Soul. It's in this state of Authentic alignment that unconditional Love pours forth from beings around you and from Source within you.

This state of being gives rise to a Vibrational resonance that will align you with ideas to create the New Earth. Technologies that encourage more Love, more Light and more Expansion on this planet. Your natural Authentic State of Being is one that can call forth any new creation at will, can ask the question: What inventions can I bring forth to illuminate this New Earth further now?"

From a natural state of Authenticity Source will shower you with Unconditional Love for asking the question. What comes after that is floods of light codes into your awareness that give you access to the Full knowing of what is to be created into form for the planet now. What you can create with your Creator self to illuminate you and others deeply?

This is your source given power, this rests at the depth of your soul and awakens naturally when you are aligned body, mind and heart.

Breathe into this alignment now. Breathe deeply into the facets of your Bravery for being so Authentic with yourself, see yourself sinking into such a depth of alignment that you move forth as your highest self, embodied in human form.

This is your divine right, and this vibration gives way to new light to shape, new ways of thinking, new front lines of expansion.

You are the creator of the new world and it's through Authenticity this happens naturally. Stand in this now, allow the light of this Star Gate to seep deeper and deeper into you now. Allow this Authentic

Embodiment to awaken from within.

Breathe and absorb this state."

This Star Gate leaves trails of magic for you to find. Write in your journal any question you wish as if your journal was a magical genie lamp and know that if asked from a state of True Authentic Alignment of Heart, Mind and Body with the Soul you will enter into the Power of this Star Gate in the depths of your own cells and awaken to Visions of the New Earth and what you can bring Forth now! For you and for us all!

Love you.

Star Gate 9- Anchor into the Physical

Allow what you experienced to pour onto these pages. As you shape this light into form by writing it on these pages you begin to Embody this Wisdom in your own Temple. Once you reach Embodiment this Wisdom is Awakened inside of you. Writing is your first step into Embodiment.

NAKED STARSEED

Star Gate 10
LOVE

Star Gate of Love, of melting back into your true essence, one with Source Creator. I invite you to get cozy for this Star Gate. This Star Gate will be one of melting, relaxing, deeply sinking into the depth of what you're made of, LOVE.

Story time Star Gate, welcome to an illuminated ring of Divine Love and unconditional envelopment into Bliss.

"I am inside you already, you are walking through me in the version of a ring of light, however I am also the very matter you are built from. Love, the feeling of being connected to all things in all moments is what you are, and what I am.

You were created to feel love, to emanate love and dance in the witness of Love. You are here to Embody the warrior essence of Love, to Embody the sweetness of Love, to Embody all facets of love and expression. This topic can never be separated from you as you are the topic of Love. It's this very unfolding onto oneself that allows you to Spiral back into the depth of your own embodied magic!

Journey with me into the envelopment of Love now. Feel into your body, tune into the sensations of how your body feels resting upon this earth plane. You are connected to the Earth at this time are you not? Feel into the depths of this connection, and begin to follow this sensation with a curious container. Your connected to the floor underneath you. The floor is connected to the earth. The earth is connected to the trees and flowers growing up around you, connected to the other buildings and cities around you. Connected to the electric poles, the dogs running about and the food being served in diners. Connected to all at once, and you are connected to this connection now.

This is Love, this knowing of connection to all things and feeling the rhythm of all things inside of you and outside of you. This view point inspires love to spring forth from within, as it aligns you with your Ascended Master Self that has awakened the Remembrance from within of true connection to all things.

How does this knowing feel inside of your heart? Do you feel expanded knowing that everything is interconnected? Does this expansion feel like love?

Every time you expand you are embodying more of this loving light, it's this embodiment that is love, it is you that is love and it is what you shall create that is built of you, which is love.   There is nothing that you could do that would ever separate you from Love, nothing. You will always be receiving more and more of this expanded light and you will always be sharing more and more of your illuminated self, this is all Source love. Source is the essence of all things, which is Love.

If there could be one thing that you could give yourself in order to feel this connection deeper what would that be?

Gift yourself that in a vision now...This is Love.

Love is at your service always, love is here to lift you, inspire you, envelope you in bliss. Love is here to hold you, align you and awaken you to deeper knowledge of self-power.

Love is the Gate Way to Ascended Mastery for it envelops all that we do when we move through a state of Authenticity. When our Mind is aligned with our heart which is aligned with our body we are being Authentic which draws closer our Highest self into embodiment. This is all enveloped in Love for self when one moves into this state of

Alignment. Are you beginning to see how love is not separate from you or anything you do?

Sink into a light cocoon of light, one that comes in through your crown and is tethered to the Earth's core crystal. Allow all the illumination you just walked through to be imbedded into the depths of your cells now. Allow yourself to rest in this vision for as long as you choose amplifying your awareness of the love inside of you."

Rest. Drink tons of water and take a rose quartz crystal bath with sea salts to fully integrate this Star Gate if you feel called. As you drop the Rose Quartz into the tub ask each crystal to further this embodiment with you, ask the water to awaken each ounce of love in every cell of your being and YOU become the creator of the love you feel in each moment. You become the Divine love activator of self.

I love you.

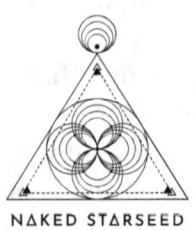

Star Gate 10- Anchor into the Physical

Allow what you experienced to pour onto these pages. As you shape this light into form by writing it on these pages you begin to Embody this Wisdom in your own Temple. Once you reach Embodiment this Wisdom is Awakened inside of you. Writing is your first step into Embodiment.

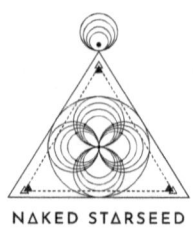

NΔKED STΔRSEED

Star Gate 11
Mastery - Create your own Star Gates

Ring of Star Light standing before you. This pulsating ring of light is larger than all of the other Star Gates you have walked through. This Star Gate is larger because it contains the Mastery Remembrance that is YOU. It is a Living Activation that will awaken the last bits of your DNA into a state of Mastery.

This Star Gate has been known to unlock your many hidden gifts, amplify your powerful Magnet of Abundance and Reconnect you back to self. You will feel called to unplug from external sources of input and flex the muscle of channeling your own deep inner wisdom from the inside of your being.

In each and every one of your cells contains the wisdom, knowing and gifts of everything in this Multi Verse. EVERYTHING is Inside of you now, and EVERYTHING is ready to awaken now.

Take a few deep breathes and fully come into your body before you walk through this Star Gate. Set up Sacred Space, burn smoke and allow the trails of magic to float to the stars. Get your Favorite rock or Crystal and allow what you love to be close to you for this Star Gate Ceremony.

Gather your favorite tea, get on a nice outfit that enhances your Glow from within and prepare to Awaken, then Embody the Mastery on the other side of this Star Gate.

Breathe deeply into this Sacred setting. Take your time. Make an evening out of it, bath yourself, do your hair and prepare. Hold I your mind's eye the Ascended Mastery Vision of all that is you and prepare to honor this Imprint and Integrate into your Physical while you walk through this Star Gate.

YOU are the only one who can awaken this Mastery inside of your being, YOU are the only one that can Embody this level of Remembrance for yourself, so see it. YOU seeing it is YOU calling it to be into form now.

Ready Love? After this, you will never be small in the perceptual image of self, again.

"Many think I guide from above. I do not. Some ponder about me guiding from the Earth, I do not. Do you know where I guide from? I guide from the center of all that is YOU.

You are the anchor to Ascension; the cells of your body are the Gate ways to Full Remembrance. The Power, Wisdom, Healing Gifts and Magical Powers are all being drawn out into the light from within YOU. Without you, there would be no Mystical Gifts available, no Power to wield more light and no Mastery to step into.

This opportunity is here because You are here and it is from within YOU this last Star Gate shall be revealed.

From deep within your Awakened Cells I call forth this Illuminated Star Gate. Breathe Deeply as this ring of light comes forth into the Inner Eye of the Mind.

Witness before you this Star Gate of Self Mastery, a ring of light for you to step through for the Final Spiral Step back to self within. This ring of light is YOU Glowing in all of your Source Origins. Burning Bright and fully encapsulated and grounded into your Human Form. Your Human Form is the Temple for this wisdom to express itself.

As you merge your human form with this ring of light I ask you to breathe deeply, tap the parts of your body that long for more light and massage the awareness of your own inner Temple deep into your being now. All the while breathing deeply into your belly.

Take as much time as you need to allow this process to naturally flow through you then pick the book back up when you're ready to proceed.

This Full Remembrance ring of perfection you just called forth from within yourself has illuminated this entire world. You have just upgraded you, you have also just upgraded the level of light on this planet as a whole.

You are the answers you seek, you are the light you long for, you are the Master of Ascension here to Guide others back to the Power within themselves. It is YOU.

I SEE YOU. I FEEL YOU. I LOVE YOU. I AM YOU."

The tingles of light perfection bouncing through you are ecstatic, they play upon what you are and dance with shaping the light around you. Whatever you wish IS, your light body will create a reflection in your outer world which will give you whatever it is you Wish to Create.

Shape the Light, Love the Mastery that is YOU and Dance in this Cosmic Realm of PLAY while we all Ascend into Full Alignment with the Seed of Source within.

I love you.

NAKED STARSEED

Star Gate 11 – Anchor into the Physical

The Following Pages are for you to Create your own Star Gates to walk through. Ponder the Rings of Light and what you wish to Call Forth, then allow the Visions to Flood You.

Write those Visions here and anchor them into the Earthly Realms Creating your Own Multi-Dimensional Pathway!

NΔKED STΔRSEED

Naked Starseed® Mystery School

Sacred Container for Ascension Mastery

Created in 2021 as a Pyramid of Light Scarlet was ordained as the Naked Starseed Portal of Light by her Star Family. This opened up visions of Star Gates that came flooding through to channel the Naked Starseed® Mystery School.

This is a Sacred Container where Scarlet shares Videos of her Channeling the Star Gates to give you Visions of Remembrance and create Awakenings for other Light Beings to step into their Ascended Mastery. Inside the school Light Beings can ask Scarlet questions and receive mini-readings as well as Activate new Visions to be Channeled through Scarlet.

When you are a Student and you ask a questions, this question activates consciousness expansion and that expansion will come through Scarlet in the form of a Vision which she will then share to add more light to this Planet.

You are welcome to join at any time and become a part of this community of Light Walkers. The container is a living Morphic Field that is set up to Awaken your Inner Gifts, Your Inner Remembrance so that you can go out and Shape the Light around you to create the life you Dream of Living.

You are the creator being that created this entire Multiverse, once you Embody that knowing you will have the Power to Shape the Light into form around you, travel to Any Where in the World at the Speed of Light and Create new Worlds.

Become the Innovative Light Being you came here to become, the Energy on Earth at this time is ripe for this Ascension.

Join us at https://www.patreon.com/nakedstarseed

www.nakedstarseed.com

Scarlet Ravin – *Naked Starseed®*

I would like to share a little bit more about me with you. As each Mystery school popping up on this planet will all have different flavors to them according to who that Channel is. We all have different gifts and by me sharing my specific gifts with you, you will have a deeper look into what this Naked Starseed® Mystery School will Feel like.

I am a Visionary. What this means is that I have Visions being shown to me by other Star Family Beings which will being more light and growth to the Beings on this Planet. I am a Starseed, I have a Star Family living in the Galaxies sharing higher Visions with me so we can upgrade Earth and Earth's People to a new level of Consciousness. This is Evolution.

My soul mission is to Channel in this light and help with this Ascension Process we are all in now. The Visions I am shared are specific to me and my gifts and my Mission. They will attract in like vibrational light beings to join the Mystery School and gift them the light waves to Remember their own Mission and carry that forward.

The Beings that join the Mystery School will help in bringing more light through me and also Inspire more Evolution for all. We are all one Fabric of light working as one showing up as a unique expression.

I am given Ancient Technology Visions, this means that I have been shown how to make Technologies that Heal anything and bring forward the Remembrance of our relationship between the Earth and Stars. I have been taught how to harness this energy into a Chamber so beings can go in the Chamber and upgrade their Body, Mind and Soul by reestablishing this connection. The First Star Chamber is currently being built now from these Visions.

I am an Alchemist. My Temple Body is a portal in which I transmute energy through me back to the light. I also do this externally with Plant Medicine and Earth Medicine. My company White Fox Medicine is a channeled company with formulas from Star Wisdom. I speak to the plants and spirits and create formulas that add more light to this planet and are customized to what the collective needs most at that time.

You can see more of my Alchemy at www.whitefoxnectars.com and www.whitefoxatmospheres.com

I am also connected to Psilocybin. I work with the spirits of Psilocybin as they are Intergalactic Beings connected to the Galactic Counsel. I create Psilocybin alchemy to grow more light in the brain and inspire more joy and I also alchemize deeper journey formulas to transmute density to light as if it were a lightning bolt.

I have channeled a book from the Spirit of Psilocybin that shares 10 great teachings from them and inspires a deeper connection to the heart of the medicine.

You can see more about that at www.psilocybinlovemedicine.com

I have been a channel and medicine woman since birth. I offer readings where I share the visions of your light body back to you. You can also receive a mini session from me when you join the Naked Starseed® Mystery School Ascension Container.

I speak to the plants and spirits and they share with me about their connection to all and inspire me to feel that within myself. I am an HSP, Highly Sensitive Person and I require much time alone, in nature and with my animals. I love silence because for me the space is never empty. It is always filled with vibrations of all that is around me and I feel that in my body as if I am hearing it in my ears.

I speak to my animals and they speak back, we share gifts with one another and commune in a state of love. They are a huge anchor for me to this planet as I relate to them so deeply and they see me so deeply I feel very Soul Fed by animals.

I started Naked Starseed® to take my next step into my new chapter of the Mystery School. I wanted to show people a deeper look at HOW I live so that insight may inspire them to live back in a state of wholeness. I live in Harmony with Nature and my Powers. It is from this place I move through this world. I am a Multidimensional Super Hero.

Naked Starseed® will SHOW you how I live, which for me is also very vulnerable to show you. I am a very private person and I love to be solo. My growth is around showing the world all of me in all of my glory now. I will slowly unveil my layers and how I see this world slowly. That is why I called it "Naked" Starseed. To me Naked means no more hiding my True Self, no more covering up my natural beauty, no more veils of any kind, including clothing.

To totally Strip back down to the Natural, Naked Canvas of Light with zero limiting beliefs, zero traumas, just pure Ascended Mastery Naked in all its glory!

Together we will strip back the layers of hiding, we will allow more and more of our natural light to shine forth and we will bask in this illumination now!

Mystery School Platform is

https://www.patreon.com/nakedstarseed

Naked Starseed®

www.nakedstarseed.com

Scarlet Ravin

www.scarletravin.com

Thank you for tuning into me and my offerings. I am exciting to Join you in the collective Ascension and to Shape this light into an entirely new world!

Love you.

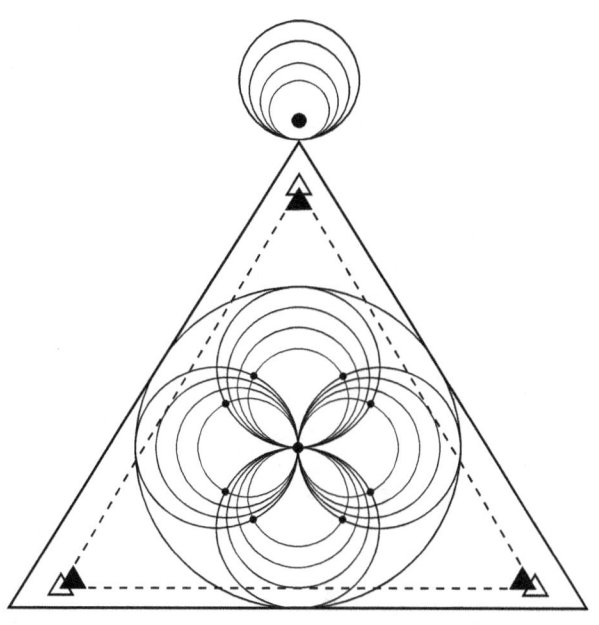

NAKED STARSEED

www.ingramcontent.com/pod-product-compliance
Lightning Source LLC
Chambersburg PA
CBHW051457290426
44109CB00016B/1792